What Do You Do?

poems by

Kathryn Donohue

Finishing Line Press
Georgetown, Kentucky

What Do You Do?

Copyright © 2018 by Kathryn Donohue
ISBN 978-1-63534-722-7 First Edition
All rights reserved under International and Pan-American Copyright Conventions.
No part of this book may be reproduced in any manner whatsoever without written permission from the publisher, except in the case of brief quotations embodied in critical articles and reviews.

ACKNOWLEDGMENTS

Thank you to the journals where versions of these poems originally appeared:

"When we tell the story of us right now" appeared in *American Chordata*
"Where are you from?" "How old are you?" and "Jamaica Stories" appeared in *Gettysburg Review*
"What happened? (To a Young Traveler)" appeared in *Hunger Mountain*
"Indonesia Stories" appeared in *MiPOesias*
"What might have happened" appeared in *Typo*
"What do you do" and "Brazil Stories" appeared in *Newtown Literary*

Publisher: Leah Maines
Editor: Christen Kincaid
Cover Art: Ali Worthington and Luke Cloran
Author Photo: Anthony Agnello
Cover Design: Elizabeth Maines McCleavy

Printed in the USA on acid-free paper.
Order online: www.finishinglinepress.com
        also available on amazon.com

Author inquiries and mail orders:
Finishing Line Press
P. O. Box 1626
Georgetown, Kentucky 40324
U. S. A.

Table of Contents

When we tell the story of us right now 1

1

Where are you from? 5

How are you? 6

How old are you? 8

What do you want to do? 10

2

Pater Noster 13

3

What do you do? 17

Can I help you? 18

Where did you go?

i.   Jamaica Stories 21

ii. Brazil Stories 23

iii. Indonesia Stories 24

What happened? (To a Young Traveler) 25

What can I say? 26

What might have happened? 27

For all the people I love

When we tell the story of us right now

we'll use the words we've been given
to describe time. Like we're supposed to,

we'll say years ago, and not acknowledge
how units flicker, elide, swell

a decade into seconds and then it's not a
matter of how long, days into a barbed

valley, so before and after are terrains
that don't touch. We'll use a month

with its attendant numbers, naming a
moment remembered for how a tea kettle

can sound so abrupt, how even stocking
feet on old carpet make some soft noise.

1.

Where Are You From?

I measure the distance between here and there in hours,
the span of visits
in meals and walks and indigo blinks of a large television you can't hear
from outside. I'm from

the place my parents are from and their parents and their
parents whose parents
came from far away. Behind a brown house,
a swingset

beginning to rust, streetlamps on nearby
hills hover
below the horizon after eight o'clock at night. An old priest
told my brother

he loved Scranton, because the mountains made him think of an island
just a thousand miles
to the equator's north, where he lived until he turned
seventeen. In a valley,

it is easy to believe every eye in the world
is watching
though the center of the earth is on fire
miles beneath your feet.

I am from a place I left
a long time ago.

How are you?

Wide awake. Not pregnant. Thinking a song
I heard years ago.
Things are good. Surrounded by vapors,
nitrogen, oxygen, pollution

particulates, carbon dioxide
governed by nuclei
I can only see stained in
grainy pictures.

I am composed and ordered by exchange of amino acids.
We're fine. I promise.
We're fine. It's one of those days
when I wish

I was a gardener. In Holland, in 1637, tulips were valued
higher than gold.
Some historians say this was the first
recorded speculative

bubble—a price unhinged from intrinsic value. One of those days
when I can't decide
what's intrinsic. Every morning, I should walk straight rows
of leaves, petals,

tomatoes, green beans. Anther, filament, stigma, style, ovary, ovule,
sepal, stem.
I should chant flower anatomy at passersby
then befriend

those who smile. We're fine. We are
guarded by
history's harshest artillery, clothed, sheltered,
fed, loved, yes

loved, humming the refrain to an old show tune. We are tethered
to the ground
which spins imperceptibly. I'm here.
I'm here now.

How old are you?

I'll remain this age forever if we
never meet again.
In the region of your brain that counts fine lines
and weighs

what someone knows, I'll stay thirty-two —too young
to be president,
too old to start flying as an Air Force pilot, faster
than radar waves

that try to find me—to stop me. In *West Side Story*'s best scene,
Action tells Doc
"You was never my age." The body of a fourteen-year-old girl
is almost always

angled at that specific forward lean. I recognize it.
But I was never that age.
Heisenberg says the act of watching causes a disturbance,
so it's hard

"The more precisely the position is determined, the
less precisely
the momentum is known." Viewers release their own energy
marking our thoughts

like the sun marks skin. It's hard to answer this question
about position
and momentum. We could move undetected,
when I was young.

Not like the planes, we've surrendered stealth.
So to be fourteen
means something else now. What will it mean
to be old?

Tough lap of the track my father calls it. When your friends die
your joints get stiff.
I was promised I could be president someday. I could fly
to the moon

if I set my mind to it. Dream it and you can do it, but then
the knees start
to go. You forget how to turn on a burner or button a shirt,
but still

remember the song you and a neighbor danced to at the Spring Formal
freshman year. Then,
there was a slower fade between seasons. I remember
a colder spring.

I remember breath condensed in the blond light of an April
morning. Already,
I am old enough to have watched the weather
change.

What do you want to do?

My heroes were athletic. They could jump higher
than ever before in the fourth quarter or when someone
was in danger. Their limbs' smooth movements

were a translation of an elegant ethical code. My heroines
were better. They could find the tear at the center
of any emergency, could walk into any room

steady breath, ready hands. I'm trying.
I want to be both. I want to be the one who wins
and the one who cleans wounds. I have sometimes

arrived at the right moment, run faster, swung harder,
but I have a boss. When she says, "What do you think?" I don't answer
right away. I'm trying to improve my balance.

That's what I dream of at night. When I was young,
I wanted to dismantle the military. In one of my favorite poems,
Tomaž says, "Money is the devil." I hear him saying it.

I'd like to break the National Debt Clock—wear some color
to blend into Union Square so no one would notice when I threw
thousands of stones to explode every bulb,

to relieve the chess masters, the children screaming on the playground,
the hordes boarding the subways, to silence
the clock's refrain—*Be afraid, Be sorry.* I fall asleep thinking about my job,

counting, but I dream sometimes of the power to hover,
just a toe poised on the point of a tall building. Balance isn't a thing you
have or don't. It's a verb, a constant series of adjustments of the ankle,

the gaze, the wish to fly, the pull
to survive. I have no elegant code. I'm trying
for smooth movements.

2.

Pater Noster

On the other side of the Jabbok, our grandfather was left alone. And a man wrestled him until dawn.

Our grandfather liked his job.

He was a war hero who killed people, would wake some nights counting. He had many children. He had stippled sagging cheeks.

Our grandfather, asked about vaporized bones and teeth, aberrant chromosomes, blindness and burning, said Truman was a saint.

He never ate dessert. His favorite snack was peanuts. I remember the texture of his face.

Our grandfather would wake some nights screaming. Are we to be forgiven then?

He crossed an icy river to attack the Hessian forces.

Our grandfather was born in Salzburg to Leopold and Anna Maria. His father, for a game as it were, began to teach him the clavier. He saw Louis Armstong's gums bleed, Duke Ellington's short ringed fingers sparkle. He named for us what are the classics, said,
"Love, love, love, that is the soul of genius."
He said "I love you madly."

Our grandfather woke up very early.

Our grandfather was a salesman. Our grandfather liked his job.

He did not tolerate profanity.

Our grandfather joined the day after Pearl Harbor. He waited in line.

Our grandfather knew how to shoot a gun.

Our grandfather knew how to build a fire and play by ear. He played the ukulele. He played "I've been working on the railroad," had enough money to care for his sick wife.

Our grandfather

was the son of memory, great heir of fame, dropped bombs and shot guns, presumably hitting his mark at least once.

He had ears like a Chevrolet with the doors open.

He looks like a movie star in the sepia photographs.

Our grandfather if instead of rhyming chants and irritating cops we'd merely lain down in streets, in front of airplanes, if we'd refused to stop screaming, if I had, if to function is not necessary "It is"

Our grandfather would say, his arm extended, hand just above my head.

He was an ever-fixed mark who looks on tempests but is never shaken.

He watched the six o'clock news every night, wore a suit to church. He was always early.

Our grandfather liked his job. He was a good salesman.

Our grandfather knew how to whistle.

He called Navy Seals frogmen, remembered the summer night they scaled the sides of his boat.

Our grandfather switched from Marlboros to a pipe. Eventually, he quit.

Our grandfather's father worked in the mines.

Our grandfather hated beets.
Every Easter he gave us a hula hoop or a yoyo.

3.

What do you do?

On the worst day of your life, I said the wrong thing four times.
I brought
rice pudding, your favorite. To spare my feelings, you tried
to eat.

The word gift comes from German, to poison. Failure comes from
the Greek,
to purchase a clay butterfly at a school fundraiser and
slip it

into my coat pocket on the day she died, because you needed to
do something.

Can I help you?

i.

You can stop the bleeding, say a prayer, sit here
until the sounds of our breathing slow and sync.

You can call for reinforcements who will ask the same.
You can bake something—an old recipe with warm cinnamon, but

ii.

There is, at least, a word for wound
and a word for bandage no matter
how many kinds of cut there are.

iii.

My aunts owned a store. They had a feather duster
with real feathers. I roamed that kingdom cleaning shelves
like a real person, like people I saw on television.

The best, though, was when I stood behind the register.
These were the days of metal buttons and a bell
sounded by the drawer's movement. To everyone

who entered I asked. I was a child,
few skills to offer. I badly
wanted them to say yes.

iv.

They have an Applebees, a Rite Aid, an Abercrombie.
Stanislavsky said "Generality is the enemy of all art,"
and we've seen the definite article's death.

I have hated hospital receptionists, because
what was for me the worst thing was for them
a thing that happened after lunch. A patient, a sad story.

I'm the same, though. I hear of a hurricane's approach
and am grateful for landfall in a place
that's home to no one I know.

v.

> "Through commerce, man learns to deliberate, to be honest, to acquire manners…he would not dare make a spectacle of himself for fear of damaging his credit standing and thus society may well avoid a scandal which it might otherwise have to deplore" —Samuel Ricard

Six months after the first Foxconn explosion, a poll:
56% of Americans could not think of anything negative

about Apple. How can we deplore acquired manners
and indefinite articles, a hurricane, an explosion, a man

on the ground, a factory with poor ventilation, a
-luminum dust igniting air only sounds like a special effect,

a spectacle from a world of textures too smooth to be skin.

vi.

At the entrance to the Critical Care Ward was a desk. The woman
sitting there asked and I told her I needed your father's room number.
She turned to her files. You'd been sitting nearby and heard my voice.

As we hugged, you started to cry, and she read out the number
raising her voice to be louder than the sobs. On the drive
to the hospital, I had imagined my entrance as comfort and relief

asking "What can I do?" and you'd say "You're here."
Knowing this was stupid and impossible, I practiced my lines.
When the time came, I couldn't ask you anything.

vii.

When the time comes next time,
we won't buy a Mac, we'll pile sandbags

to stop the flood or with a wave of our hands
send a country-sized low pressure system

spinning back to sea. We'll help, or we'll say,
"I am so sorry for your loss." We'll build everyone

suits of armor, but insist inside stay soft
or we'll lay down on concrete.

We'll approach the cash register to notice
what is not general or mannered about the one

who stands there. We'll discuss the song
playing in the store, probably not beautiful,

stained with market research, catchy.
At least there is a word for

Where did you go?

i. Jamaica Stories

Mr. Brooks and Miss Edith had no children,
but there had been a steady march of youth who—when
they had nowhere else—slept on a makeshift bed

in the kitchen of the couple's two-room home. One of these
was Anna, whom they all called Dimples.
Mr. Brooks could still scale trees to cut down fruit.

His knife had a two-foot blade. Miss Edith needed
more help. She was a few years older than her
husband, whom she always called Brooks.

Dimples checked on her each afternoon. You called me
not long after dinner, a note of urgency
in your voice. For a second, I was afraid,

but you wanted to tell me how happy
Miss Edith looked with Dimples'
newest baby on her lap and her hair

being braided. You sat in the cool shadow
of a cement wall, eating just-picked oranges
while Mr. Brooks offered career advice:

"A book job or a store job," he told you. The next week,
you turned twenty-three the same day he turned
eighty and six, so you killed two chickens.

He spoke in a patois so thick the first thing
you shared was this mutual surrender: neither
would really understand what the other said. But

there were things you learned. In the fifties,
he went off island. A migrant worker in Louisiana,
the money he made he used to build his home. He loved

the US he said. It gave him all he had.
Half a century after the assassination, he still
grieved for JFK, "They killed the best one."

Dinner was so delicious, you didn't feel guilty
about the chickens. You say he reminded
you of our grandfather, because every

Sunday, he walked to church two miles
each way, because they shared a kind of half
smile, because he always called you Bugsy.

ii. Brazil Stories

You only knew *obrigada*, they thought you were quiet
and polite. You learned to crochet,
because there was no radio,

learned the language one word
at a time, making the children believe
it was a game. Eighteen,

limited to hand gestures, you got on what must have been
a small plane. Too stupid to have
been brave, you say. Your mother tried

to send care packages. They were stolen
at first, but she discovered the trick: mark the boxes
"Religious articles enclosed." With jars of

peanut butter, cereal boxes, new socks, notes
from your sisters, she included a prayer card,
so it wouldn't be a lie. St. Anthony—patron of lost things,

St. Rita—patroness of lost causes, St. Paul, whose
intercession would bring patience. You carried them
tucked between the pages of whatever book you were reading.

Letters to her were about the impossibility of French
taught in Portuguese, all the dropped stitches
in your first attempted afghan.

iii. Indonesia Stories

The woman who led you
to the largest flower on Earth claimed
to work for the government. You believed

nothing she said. She had a machete, you stopped
insisting you didn't need a guide. You describe her arm
as monstrously strong that lifted you

and each of three friends to the ledge
at the end of a path you'd never
have found: Rafflesia arnoldii.

It was there. Three feet across, the spotted
petals, a red mouth gaping, emitting the smell
of rotten meat. Like the servant

from the Wedding at Cana, who must have left that place
and announced what he'd seen every time he poured liquid,
you came back to Pittsburgh swearing.

What happened? (To a Young Traveler)

Autumn came late, and stayed for a long time.
Colors were
out of place, as trees seemed to pause.
I counted leaves

and checked temperatures as these are more easily recounted
in letters
than the sharpening taste of air. Everyone's hair got longer;
plants died.

Stripes faded as squares of sun stepped across the dining room.
Elsewhere,
there were wars, speeches, avalanches. We missed you
in the sense

that your name became a synonym for
several other things:
the miracle of flight, our concept of distance lifted from
post cards, maps,

televised expanses of ocean. We missed you
in the sense
that you were not here. The mind obscuring precise angles
of a jaw.

What can I say?

You can reach for the constitution,
an old folk song, a Beetle Bailey cartoon

or Pierre Teilhard de Chardin who said
"Always trust in the slow work." My friend Bill said

"I need fast work right now." At the end, you can say
"It is finished," but there are limited benefits

to a graceful exit. If aphorisms are like lightning,
above all the browning onion grass, lightning disappears.

Rain begins to fall. Above all,
excerpts offer comfort. Whole texts are less relaxing.

Remember what you can't explain: a perfectly dented chin.
We could write a manifesto about wanting so badly

to live up to our manifestos. Tell me
there are plenty of fish in the sea.

Plant a wooden podium between looking
and measuring. Talk about a sonata,

never mention how good it is.
Let it exist without creating for it

some stillborn fraternal twin
the song it might have been.

What might have happened?

I could have been a firefighter. I could have
taught the muscles of my neck to stay relaxed beneath a siren.
I could have learned to breathe smoke, walked into a flame.

Any minute now, I might close my eyes to admire
just the contours of calm expansive darkness.

I could have been an Atheist.
I could have been an astronaut,

but I stand here pointing to things that are not crystal or liquid to show
how they are sweet. I learned this walking out the front door of a house
that smelled like embers, with wind chimes
sounding from the back porch.

Thank you:

To Finishing Line Press for bringing this book out into the world and for all your work on behalf of poetry and poets

To the professors at the University of Pittsburgh who helped and inspired me, especially Toi Derricotte, Kathleen George, Dawn Lundy Martin, Phil Smith, and the late Tomaž Šalamun

To the writers who gave me invaluable support and feedback over the last decade and a half, especially Natasha Cahill, Robin Clarke, RB Mertz, Chana Porter, Sarah Schweig and Ryan Teitman

To The Sunnyside Writers—Virginia Arnold, Robert Browne, Nina Farrey, Dianne Franklin, Paula and Joe Snider, and the late Bob Murphy—for their friendship, generosity, and talent

To Caitlin Cassidy for the years we spent living on Woolslayer Way and for all the years since

To Rena Rifkin and Casey Talmas, who made it possible for me to become a New Yorker

To my brother, Kevin Donohue, who carried my couch down three flights of stairs while fighting a 103 degree fever

To my parents, Mike and Libby Donohue, for your patience, sacrifice, and steadfast love

To John, my favorite always

To Lyra, whose impending birth forced me to finish this book, and who is already kind and strong and brave.

Kathryn Donohue is a writer and teacher who lives in Ithaca, New York with her husband and daughter. Her poems have appeared in journals including *American Chordata, Gettysburg Review, Newtown Literary,* and *Typo Magazine.*

www.ingramcontent.com/pod-product-compliance
Lightning Source LLC
LaVergne TN
LVHW041514070426
835507LV00012B/1571